KNOWING ME, KNOWING YOU

A Biography of You and Your Loved Ones

By

C.S. Manifold

To The Point Publishing
Burke, VA

Published by:
To The Point Publishing
P.O. Box 10799
Burke, VA 22009-0799
www.CSManifold.com

ISBN 0-9748367-0-2

Library of Congress Control Number: 2004097295

DEDICATION

This book is dedicated to my loving Mother. She has always unconditionally supported and encouraged me in all of my endeavors. I would not have been able to accomplish much of what I have without her support.

The author with his mother.

ACKNOWLEDGEMENTS

Thanks to my parents for the never wavering moral support throughout the years.

Thanks to my Love, Debora, for inspiring me to be a better person every day.

Thanks to my family for being strong through tough times.

Thanks to my friends, who have always brightened my days and reminded me to enjoy life.

Thanks to the town of Hanover, PA for instilling family values.

Thanks to my friends and family who have provided feedback to me on this project, especially: Debora, Sean, Jeff, Rich, Mom, Dad, Nancy, Matt, David, Mark, Doug, and Brandon.

Thanks to Debora for being my 24-hour a day editor.

Thanks to Brent for cover layout.

Thanks to the Alzheimer's Association, and those research organizations involved in Alzheimer's research.

TABLE OF CONTENTS

PREFACE

Knowing Me, Knowing You was developed as a catalyst for the creation of "A Biography of You and Your Loved Ones."

Time does not discriminate; with the years passing by so quickly, we often forget to take a step back and realize what is important to us. This book offers us the chance to really get to know our loved ones even better, and to create a keepsake of memories for life.

When I think of my Grandmother who suffered through Alzheimer's Disease, or when I go to the nursing home to visit my Grandfather, I am reminded of everything I wish I would have done. I wish I had asked more questions, come to know them better, spent more time with them.

Now my Mother and Aunt are battling Alzheimer's and our family is attempting to come to grips with their losses of memory and communication skills. Developing this book has helped me learn more about my Mother and Aunt, but also about numerous other relatives and friends. The book has also helped me learn more about myself, by allowing me to consider other's views, beliefs, accomplishments, etc.

In searching for a way to contribute to the cause of finding the cure for Alzheimer's, I transformed my personal project of learning more about my own family and friends into a chance to contribute financially to the cause of defeating Alzheimer's Disease. The book also helps other people to create cherished memories with their loved ones. A significant portion of the profits of this book will be donated to Alzheimer's related organizations.

I hope you enjoy creating "A Biography of You and Your Loved Ones."

Alzheimer's disease causes a gradual loss of brain cells and is the leading cause of dementia. Symptoms of dementia include loss of memory and language skills, disorientation and an overall decline in the ability to think, reason, and learn. Individuals with dementia often experience anxiety, depression, and hallucinations.
For more information about the disease, or to make a donation to support research, visit the Alzheimer's Association website at www.alz.org.

INTRODUCTION

Knowing Me, Knowing You was written as a stimulus for increasing meaningful discussion between family and friends. The conversations generated by exploring this book of questions with others will result in a deep familiarization with your loved ones and yourself.

Initially, review the "Suggested Uses of the Book" section and determine how you personally will use the book. *Knowing Me, Knowing You* can be used to create a written memory of documented responses, or can simply be used to prompt great conversation between friends and family.

Determine each "Very Special Person" (VSP) in your life that you want to participate in the completion of the book. The book's owner can write responses in section "VSP 1." Let the VSP's know that they don't have to answer any questions they don't wish to. For optimal interaction, questions and responses should be reviewed and answered together, but they can be completed individually if the VSP so desires.

Once all your VSP's have finished their answers, review their responses. Have you changed your opinions on some viewpoints or beliefs? Have you developed a new perspective on your daily routine? Will you decide to try a new hobby, attend a new event, or visit a new place? Have you determined a few great gifts for each of your loved ones? Hopefully, you've shared many fond memories together!

Cherish this memento of what you and your loved ones have shared and experienced. In the end, you will have grown closer to those you love and you will likely find that you have learned not only about each other, but also about yourself.

SUGGESTED USES OF THE BOOK

As a personal biography:

Discover the real you...first when you complete the questions, and again when you see the responses of others.

As a way to really get to know the people you care about while creating memories and a keepsake for life:

- ❖ Significant Other
- ❖ Parents
- ❖ Grandparents
- ❖ Siblings
- ❖ Friends

As a way to stimulate memorable conversation:

- ❖ On a family trip
- ❖ On a long flight with a friend
- ❖ At parties with friends and family
- ❖ At family get-togethers
- ❖ When visiting someone special in the hospital or nursing home

As a great gift for anyone on any occasion:

- ❖ As a Christmas or Hanukah gift for that hard-to-buy-for person
- ❖ As a heart felt birthday gift
- ❖ For Mother's Day or Father's Day
- ❖ As a Valentines Day gift for your Love
- ❖ As a graduation gift for that special someone
- ❖ As a memorable wedding gift
- ❖ As a token gift for business associates and customers/clients

Other uses:

- ❖ As a way to get to know someone you just started dating
- ❖ As a bonding experience in Sororities and Fraternities
- ❖ As an icebreaker at church retreats
- ❖ As a way to learn what others would like for gifts
- ❖ As a way to create memories with people close to you who have Alzheimer's Disease and other memory related illnesses

WHAT'S IN IT FOR YOU

Tangibles
- ❖ A personal written autobiography
- ❖ A written biography of the people you care about most

Intangibles
- ❖ The experience of really getting to know yourself
- ❖ The experience of getting to know your loved ones better while creating new memories

Learning from others
- ❖ Expand your opinions and knowledge by hearing other's viewpoints in "Political Views," "Political Yes No," and "Beliefs"
- ❖ Become a great gift giver and discover some new indulgences in "Favorites"
- ❖ Expose yourself to great places to visit, exciting activities to enjoy, and unique experiences to be had in "Have You Ever…," "Have You Been…," "Hobbies And Pastimes," "Events of Your Life," and "Favorites"
- ❖ Compare your normal routine to the routines of others (and decide what you may want to change about your life) in "The Average Day," "Hours Per Week," and "How Many Times…"

PERSONAL INFORMATION

Complete each section as indicated. Once you have entered your name as a "Very Special Person" (VSP), use that same VSP number throughout the book. The book's owner will normally list themselves as "VSP 1."

General Information

- VSP 1: Name: _____ Signature: _____

    Birth Date: _____ Birth Location: _____

    Date Began This Book: _____ Date Finished This Book: _____

- VSP 2: Name: _____ Signature: _____

    Birth Date: _____ Birth Location: _____

    Date Began This Book: _____ Date Finished This Book: _____

- VSP 3: Name: _____ Signature: _____

    Birth Date: _____ Birth Location: _____

    Date Began This Book: _____ Date Finished This Book: _____

- VSP 4: Name: _____ Signature: _____

    Birth Date: _____ Birth Location: _____

    Date Began This Book: _____ Date Finished This Book: _____

- VSP 5: Name: _____ Signature: _____

    Birth Date: _____ Birth Location: _____

    Date Began This Book: _____ Date Finished This Book: _____

- VSP 6: Name: _____ Signature: _____

    Birth Date: _____ Birth Location: _____

    Date Began This Book: _____ Date Finished This Book: _____

Physical Information

- VSP 1: Height: _____ Weight: _____

    Hair Color: _____ Eye Color: _____

    Build: _____ Complexion: _____

    Contacts/Glasses: _____ Left or Right Handed: _____

- VSP 2: Height: _____ Weight: _____

    Hair Color: _____ Eye Color: _____

    Build: _____ _____ Complexion: _____

    Contacts/Glasses: _____ Left or Right Handed: _____

- VSP 3: Height: _____ Weight: _____

    Hair Color: _____ Eye Color: _____

    Build: _____ Complexion: _____

    Contacts/Glasses: _____ Left or Right Handed: _____

- VSP 4: Height: _____ Weight: _____

  Hair Color: _____ Eye Color: _____

  Build: _____ Complexion: _____

  Contacts/Glasses: _____ Left or Right Handed: _____

- VSP 5: Height: _____ Weight: _____

  Hair Color: _____ Eye Color: _____

  Build: _____ Complexion: _____

  Contacts/Glasses: _____ Left or Right Handed: _____

- VSP 6: Height: _____ Weight: _____

  Hair Color: _____ Eye Color: _____

  Build: _____ Complexion: _____

  Contacts/Glasses: _____ Left or Right Handed: _____

Describe any scars, tattoos, or piercings:

- VSP 1: _____

_____

- VSP 2: _____

_____

- VSP 3: _____

_____

- VSP 4: _____

_____

- VSP 5: _____

_____

- VSP 6: _____

_____

List your sizes

- VSP 1: Shirts_____ Pants_____ Shoes_____

    Other_____

- VSP 2: Shirts_____ Pants_____ Shoes_____

    Other_____

- VSP 3: Shirts_____ Pants_____ Shoes_____

    Other_____

- VSP 4: Shirts_____ Pants_____ Shoes_____

    Other_____

- VSP 5: Shirts_____ Pants_____ Shoes_____

    Other_____

- VSP 6: Shirts_____ Pants_____ Shoes_____

    Other_____

Describe your dress style (clothing, footwear, jewelry, headwear, accessories, etc.):

- VSP 1: _____

_____

- VSP 2: _____

_____

- VSP 3: _____

_____

- VSP 4: _____

_____

- VSP 5: _____

_____

- VSP 6: _____

_____

What do you think are your best and worst physical features?

- VSP 1: best: _____ worst: _____
- VSP 2: best: _____ worst: _____
- VSP 3: best: _____ worst: _____
- VSP 4: best: _____ worst: _____
- VSP 5: best: _____ worst: _____
- VSP 6: best: _____ worst: _____

What celebrities have you been told you physically resemble?

- VSP 1: _____
- VSP 2: _____
- VSP 3: _____
- VSP 4: _____
- VSP 5: _____
- VSP 6: _____

List your current and past nicknames (as a child and as an adult):

- VSP 1: _____
- VSP 2: _____
- VSP 3: _____
- VSP 4: _____
- VSP 5: _____
- VSP 6: _____

What high school did you attend?

- VSP 1: _____
- VSP 2: _____
- VSP 3: _____
- VSP 4: _____
- VSP 5: _____
- VSP 6: _____

List any colleges or other advanced schooling:

- VSP 1: _____
- VSP 2: _____
- VSP 3: _____
- VSP 4: _____
- VSP 5: _____
- VSP 6: _____

What is your heritage (1/4 German, 3/4 English, etc)?

- VSP 1: _____
- VSP 2: _____
- VSP 3: _____
- VSP 4: _____
- VSP 5: _____
- VSP 6: _____

Comment on your job/career (description, if you like it, etc.):

- VSP 1: _____

_____

- VSP 2: _____

_____

- VSP 3: _____

_____

- VSP 4: _____

_____

- VSP 5: _____

_____

- VSP 6: _____

_____

PERSONALITY

List three important events in your life that have shaped who you are today! Explain your answer.

- VSP 1: _____

_____

- VSP 2: _____

_____

- VSP 3: _____

_____

- VSP 4: _____

_____

- VSP 5: _____

_____

- VSP 6: _____

_____

List your five best personality traits:

- VSP 1: _____
- VSP 2: _____
- VSP 3: _____
- VSP 4: _____
- VSP 5: _____
- VSP 6: _____

List your three worst personality traits:

- VSP 1: _____
- VSP 2: _____
- VSP 3: _____
- VSP 4: _____
- VSP 5: _____
- VSP 6: _____

Describe something you have done (or didn't do) that you regret:

- VSP 1: _____
- VSP 2: _____
- VSP 3: _____
- VSP 4: _____
- VSP 5: _____
- VSP 6: _____

List things you fear or worry about:

- VSP 1: _____
- VSP 2: _____
- VSP 3: _____
- VSP 4: _____
- VSP 5: _____
- VSP 6: _____

What makes you sad or makes you cry?

- VSP 1: _____

_____

- VSP 2: _____

_____

- VSP 3: _____

_____

- VSP 4: _____

_____

- VSP 5: _____

_____

- VSP 6: _____

_____

What makes you happy or makes you smile or laugh?

- VSP 1: _____

_____

- VSP 2: _____

_____

- VSP 3: _____

_____

- VSP 4: _____

_____

- VSP 5: _____

_____

- VSP 6: _____

_____

Have you stolen something worth over $10? If so, what?

- VSP 1: _____
- VSP 2: _____
- VSP 3: _____
- VSP 4: _____
- VSP 5: _____
- VSP 6: _____

Have you stolen something worth under $10? If so, what?

- VSP 1: _____
- VSP 2: _____
- VSP 3: _____
- VSP 4: _____
- VSP 5: _____
- VSP 6: _____

List your most prized possessions:

- VSP 1: _____

_____

- VSP 2: _____

_____

- VSP 3: _____

_____

- VSP 4: _____

_____

- VSP 5: _____

_____

- VSP 6: _____

_____

FAMILY AND FRIENDS

List three important family members, alive or deceased. Include their name, relation to you, and at least five words that describe that person:

- VSP 1: _____

_____

_____

_____

- VSP 2: _____

_____

_____

_____

- VSP 3: _____

_____

_____

_____

- VSP 4: _____

_____

_____

_____

- VSP 5: _____

_____

_____

_____

- VSP 6: _____

_____

_____

_____

List three important friends from over the years and include at least five words that describe that person:

- VSP 1: _____

_____

_____

_____

- VSP 2: _____

_____

_____

_____

- VSP 3: _____

_____

_____

_____

- VSP 4: _____

_____

_____

_____

- VSP 5: _____

_____

_____

_____

- VSP 6: _____

_____

_____

_____

List people who have influenced you and describe how they have influenced you:

- VSP 1: _____

  _____

- VSP 2: _____

  _____

- VSP 3: _____

  _____

- VSP 4: _____

  _____

- VSP 5: _____

  _____

- VSP 6: _____

  _____

What five qualities do you look for in a friend?

- VSP 1: _____
- VSP 2: _____
- VSP 3: _____
- VSP 4: _____
- VSP 5: _____
- VSP 6: _____

Describe the qualities of a good romantic relationship:

- VSP 1: _____
- VSP 2: _____
- VSP 3: _____
- VSP 4: _____
- VSP 5: _____
- VSP 6: _____

Describe what you look(ed) for in your significant other:

- VSP 1: _____

  _____

- VSP 2: _____

  _____

- VSP 3: _____

  _____

- VSP 4: _____

  _____

- VSP 5: _____

  _____

- VSP 6: _____

  _____

How did you meet your significant other?

- VSP 1: _____

_____

- VSP 2: _____

_____

- VSP 3: _____

_____

- VSP 4: _____

_____

- VSP 5: _____

_____

- VSP 6: _____

_____

Describe your engagement proposal:

- VSP 1: _____

_____

- VSP 2: _____

_____

- VSP 3: _____

_____

- VSP 4: _____

_____

- VSP 5: _____

_____

- VSP 6: _____

_____

Describe your wedding day:

- VSP 1: _____

_____

- VSP 2: _____

_____

- VSP 3: _____

_____

- VSP 4: _____

_____

- VSP 5: _____

_____

- VSP 6: _____

_____

Describe your honeymoon:

- VSP 1: _____

_____

- VSP 2: _____

_____

- VSP 3: _____

_____

- VSP 4: _____

_____

- VSP 5: _____

_____

- VSP 6: _____

_____

Describe the day your children were born:

- VSP 1: _____

_____

- VSP 2: _____

_____

- VSP 3: _____

_____

- VSP 4: _____

_____

- VSP 5: _____

_____

- VSP 6: _____

_____

HOBBIES AND PASTIMES

List your favorite childhood playtime activities:

- VSP 1: _____

_____

- VSP 2: _____

_____

- VSP 3: _____

_____

- VSP 4: _____

_____

- VSP 5: _____

_____

- VSP 6: _____

_____

List your favorite school subjects (K-12):

- VSP 1: _____
- VSP 2: _____
- VSP 3: _____
- VSP 4: _____
- VSP 5: _____
- VSP 6: _____

List your least favorite school subjects (K-12):

- VSP 1: _____
- VSP 2: _____
- VSP 3: _____
- VSP 4: _____
- VSP 5: _____
- VSP 6: _____

List school extracurricular activities/sports/organizations in which you participated (K-12):

- VSP 1: _____

_____

- VSP 2: _____

_____

- VSP 3: _____

_____

- VSP 4: _____

_____

- VSP 5: _____

_____

- VSP 6: _____

_____

Describe your college pastimes/activities:

- VSP 1: _____

_____

- VSP 2: _____

_____

- VSP 3: _____

_____

- VSP 4: _____

_____

- VSP 5: _____

_____

- VSP 6: _____

_____

List your adult pastimes/activities/hobbies/collections/memberships, etc.:

- VSP 1: _____

_____

- VSP 2: _____

_____

- VSP 3: _____

_____

- VSP 4: _____

_____

- VSP 5: _____

_____

- VSP 6: _____

_____

ACCOMPLISHMENTS AND SKILLS

Rate yourself on a scale of 1-10 (10 being best.)

	VSP#	1	2	3	4	5	6
Athletics		——	——	——	——	——	——
Creativity		——	——	——	——	——	——
Mechanical Inclination		——	——	——	——	——	——
Math		——	——	——	——	——	——
Grammar/Vocabulary		——	——	——	——	——	——
Communicating		——	——	——	——	——	——
Listening		——	——	——	——	——	——
Interpersonal Skills (getting along with others)		——	——	——	——	——	——
Technology/Computers		——	——	——	——	——	——
Dancing		——	——	——	——	——	——
Singing		——	——	——	——	——	——
Cooking		——	——	——	——	——	——

List special talents you possess:

- VSP 1: _____

_____

- VSP 2: _____

_____

- VSP 3: _____

_____

- VSP 4: _____

_____

- VSP 5: _____

_____

- VSP 6: _____

_____

Do you speak another language? If so, what language and what is your proficiency?

- VSP 1: _____
- VSP 2: _____
- VSP 3: _____
- VSP 4: _____
- VSP 5: _____
- VSP 6: _____

List sports in which you do well:

- VSP 1: _____
- VSP 2: _____
- VSP 3: _____
- VSP 4: _____
- VSP 5: _____
- VSP 6: _____

What is your best golf score? What is your average on a 72 Par course?

- VSP 1: _____
- VSP 2: _____
- VSP 3: _____
- VSP 4: _____
- VSP 5: _____
- VSP 6: _____

What is your best bowling score? What do you average?

- VSP 1: _____
- VSP 2: _____
- VSP 3: _____
- VSP 4: _____
- VSP 5: _____
- VSP 6: _____

Have you ever acted (in a play, movie, etc.)? If so, list titles and roles.

- VSP 1: _____
- VSP 2: _____
- VSP 3: _____
- VSP 4: _____
- VSP 5: _____
- VSP 6: _____

Have you ever played a musical instrument with some degree of skill? If so, expand:

- VSP 1: _____
- VSP 2: _____
- VSP 3: _____
- VSP 4: _____
- VSP 5: _____
- VSP 6: _____

List awards/contests you have won:

- VSP 1: _____

_____

- VSP 2: _____

_____

- VSP 3: _____

_____

- VSP 4: _____

_____

- VSP 5: _____

_____

- VSP 6: _____

_____

Have you ever written poetry, a story, a book, a play, music, etc? If so, was it published?

- VSP 1: _____

_____

- VSP 2: _____

_____

- VSP 3: _____

_____

- VSP 4: _____

_____

- VSP 5: _____

_____

- VSP 6: _____

_____

HISTORY IN LISTS

List places you have lived and how old you were when you lived there. (Example: Hanover, PA 1-18 yrs. and 22-24 yrs., Shippensburg, PA 19-21 yrs., Philadelphia, PA 25 yrs., Atlanta, GA 26 yrs., Washington, DC 27 yrs.-present):

- VSP 1: _____

  _____

- VSP 2: _____

  _____

- VSP 3: _____

  _____

- VSP 4: _____

  _____

- VSP 5: _____

  _____

- VSP 6: _____

  _____

List your favorite pets including their name and species, and how old you were when you owned them. [Example: Hogan(dog) 4-5 yrs., Snoopy(dog) 13-27 yrs.]:

- VSP 1: _____

_____

- VSP 2: _____

_____

- VSP 3: _____

_____

- VSP 4: _____

_____

- VSP 5: _____

_____

- VSP 6: _____

_____

Describe your lifetime travel. (Example: I vacation twice per year and also travel on business. I have been to 46 of the 50 states. I have been to California & Florida each about ten times. I go to the beach two weekends a month during the summer. I have been to Europe three times including England, Italy, Germany, the Netherlands, and Spain.):

- VSP 1: _____

_____

_____

_____

- VSP 2: _____

_____

_____

_____

- VSP 3: _____

_____

_____

_____

- VSP 4: _____

_____

_____

_____

- VSP 5: _____

_____

_____

_____

- VSP 6: _____

_____

_____

_____

List your most influential jobs, including the name of your employer and how old you were when you were employed there. [Example: Hardee's(cook) 15-18 yrs., Ernst & Young(business consultant) 22-24 yrs., Akzo Nobel(business consultant) 25-27 yrs., ehats.com, Inc.(V.P. of Finance) 28 yrs., MACRO(Executive Director) 29-32 yrs.]:

- VSP 1: _____

_____

_____

_____

- VSP 2: _____

_____

_____

_____

- VSP 3: _____

_____

_____

_____

- VSP 4: _____

_____

_____

_____

- VSP 5: _____

_____

_____

_____

- VSP 6: _____

_____

_____

_____

List your major romantic relationships. Including their name, and how old you were when you were involved. (Jen 19-24 yrs., Michelle 24 yrs., Paris 25-26 yrs., Aries 28-29 yrs., Debora 30 yrs.-present):

- VSP 1: _____

_____

- VSP 2: _____

_____

- VSP 3: _____

_____

- VSP 4: _____

_____

- VSP 5: _____

_____

- VSP 6: _____

_____

List major medical conditions, injuries, broken bones, surgeries, stitches, hospital stays, etc.:

- VSP 1: _____

  _____

- VSP 2: _____

  _____

- VSP 3: _____

  _____

- VSP 4: _____

  _____

- VSP 5: _____

  _____

- VSP 6: _____

  _____

List volunteer work you have performed or contributions to charity:

- VSP 1: _____

_____

- VSP 2: _____

_____

- VSP 3: _____

_____

- VSP 4: _____

_____

- VSP 5: _____

_____

- VSP 6: _____

_____

EVENTS OF YOUR LIFE

List performing arts you have attended in your lifetime including concerts, opera's, plays, musicals, etc.:

- VSP 1: _____

_____

- VSP 2: _____

_____

- VSP 3: _____

_____

- VSP 4: _____

_____

- VSP 5: _____

_____

- VSP 6: _____

_____

List sporting events you have attended in your lifetime including NASCAR, WWE, NBA, NFL, MLB, NHL, major college, etc.:

- VSP 1: _____

_____

- VSP 2: _____

_____

- VSP 3: _____

_____

- VSP 4: _____

_____

- VSP 5: _____

_____

- VSP 6: _____

_____

Have you ever met someone famous? If so, describe:

- VSP 1: _____

_____

- VSP 2: _____

_____

- VSP 3: _____

_____

- VSP 4: _____

_____

- VSP 5: _____

_____

- VSP 6: _____

_____

Have you ever appeared in or attended the taping of a television show or movie? If so, describe:

- VSP 1: _____

  _____

- VSP 2: _____

  _____

- VSP 3: _____

  _____

- VSP 4: _____

  _____

- VSP 5: _____

  _____

- VSP 6: _____

  _____

List any traumatic events you have experienced including car accidents, robberies, house fires, assaults, etc.:

- VSP 1: _____

_____

- VSP 2: _____

_____

- VSP 3: _____

_____

- VSP 4: _____

_____

- VSP 5: _____

_____

- VSP 6: _____

_____

MEMORIES

Describe three childhood memories:

- VSP 1: _____

_____

_____

_____

- VSP 2: _____

_____

_____

_____

- VSP 3: _____

_____

_____

_____

- VSP 4: _____

_____

_____

_____

- VSP 5: _____

_____

_____

_____

- VSP 6: _____

_____

_____

_____

Describe three teen memories:

- VSP 1: _____

_____

_____

_____

- VSP 2: _____

_____

_____

_____   _____

- VSP 3: _____

_____

_____

_____

- VSP 4: _____

_____

_____

_____

- VSP 5: _____

_____

_____

_____

- VSP 6: _____

_____

_____

_____

Describe three memories from your twenties:

- VSP 1: _____

_____

_____

_____

- VSP 2: _____

_____

_____

_____

- VSP 3: _____

_____

_____

_____

- VSP 4: _____

_____

_____

_____

- VSP 5: _____

_____

_____

_____

- VSP 6: _____

_____

_____

_____

Describe three memories from your thirties and beyond:

- VSP 1: _____
  _____
  _____
  _____

- VSP 2: _____
  _____
  _____
  _____

- VSP 3: _____
  _____
  _____
  _____

- VSP 4: _____

_____

_____

_____

- VSP 5: _____

_____

_____

_____

- VSP 6: _____

_____

_____

_____

What is/are the best gift(s) you have ever received?

- VSP 1: _____
- VSP 2: _____
- VSP 3: _____
- VSP 4: _____
- VSP 5: _____
- VSP 6: _____

What have you dressed up as for Halloween?

- VSP 1: _____
- VSP 2: _____
- VSP 3: _____
- VSP 4: _____
- VSP 5: _____
- VSP 6: _____

What is the nicest thing anyone has ever said to you?

- VSP 1: _____
- VSP 2: _____
- VSP 3: _____
- VSP 4: _____
- VSP 5: _____
- VSP 6: _____

What is the best advise you have ever received?

- VSP 1: _____
- VSP 2: _____
- VSP 3: _____
- VSP 4: _____
- VSP 5: _____
- VSP 6: _____

What have been the three best days or moments of your life?

- VSP 1: _____

_____

- VSP 2: _____

_____

- VSP 3: _____

_____

- VSP 4: _____

_____

- VSP 5: _____

_____

- VSP 6: _____

_____

THE AVERAGE DAY

List 5-10 things you do on an average weekend. (Example: mow the grass, watch football, go to the beach, go out to dinner with my wife, go visit my parents/kids, go golfing):

- VSP 1: _____

_____

- VSP 2: _____

_____

- VSP 3: _____

_____

- VSP 4: _____

_____

- VSP 5: _____

_____

- VSP 6: _____

_____

Describe your average weekday. (Example: wake up at 6am, shower, commute ½ hour to work, work from 8am-5pm, eat lunch at my desk, drive home, cook dinner and eat with my wife, watch television with my wife, handle paperwork, go to bed by 11pm):

- VSP 1: _____

_____

_____

_____

- VSP 2: _____

_____

_____

_____

- VSP 3: _____

_____

_____

_____

- VSP 4: _____

_____

_____

_____

- VSP 5: _____

_____

_____

_____

- VSP 6: _____

_____

_____

_____

What do you think about when you first wake up in the morning?

- VSP 1: _____
- VSP 2: _____
- VSP 3: _____
- VSP 4: _____
- VSP 5: _____
- VSP 6: _____

Do you usually remember your dreams? If so, what do you dream about?

- VSP 1: _____
- VSP 2: _____
- VSP 3: _____
- VSP 4: _____
- VSP 5: _____
- VSP 6: _____

Describe your typical breakfast:

- VSP 1: _____
- VSP 2: _____
- VSP 3: _____
- VSP 4: _____
- VSP 5: _____
- VSP 6: _____

Do you daydream? What do you daydream about?

- VSP 1: _____
- VSP 2: _____
- VSP 3: _____
- VSP 4: _____
- VSP 5: _____
- VSP 6: _____

HOURS PER WEEK

Answer the number of hours per week you spend…

	VSP#	1	2	3	4	5	6
Sleeping		——	——	——	——	——	——
Commuting to and from work		——	——	——	——	——	——
Working		——	——	——	——	——	——
Emailing (not at work)		——	——	——	——	——	——
Surfing the Net (not at work)		——	——	——	——	——	——
Doing house work / yard work		——	——	——	——	——	——
Reading books/newspapers/magazines		——	——	——	——	——	——
Practicing religion (Church/Bible, etc.)		——	——	——	——	——	——
Shopping		——	——	——	——	——	——
Attending entertainment events (movies/concerts, etc.)		——	——	——	——	——	——

	VSP#	1	2	3	4	5	6
Eating		——	——	——	——	——	——
Clubbing/going to bars		——	——	——	——	——	——
Playing with your pets		——	——	——	——	——	——
Playing with your kids		——	——	——	——	——	——
Spending quiet time with your significant other		——	——	——	——	——	——
Visiting family and friends		——	——	——	——	——	——
Talking on the phone (not at work)		——	——	——	——	——	——
Paying the bills/finances		——	——	——	——	——	——
Watching TV/Videos/DVD's		——	——	——	——	——	——
Playing video games		——	——	——	——	——	——
Working on hobbies		——	——	——	——	——	——
Participating in sports or working out		——	——	——	——	——	——
Total hours accounted for (168 maximum):		——	——	——	——	——	——

HOW MANY TIMES...

	VSP#	1	2	3	4	5	6

Answer the number of times per week you...

Brush your teeth		——	——	——	——	——	——
Make your bed		——	——	——	——	——	——
Shower or bathe		——	——	——	——	——	——
Exercise		——	——	——	——	——	——
Drink alcohol		——	——	——	——	——	——

Answer the number of times per month you...

Change the sheets on your bed		——	——	——	——	——	——
Clean the house, including vacuuming and dusting		——	——	——	——	——	——
Eat fast food		——	——	——	——	——	——
Eat out (sit down)		——	——	——	——	——	——
Go to church		——	——	——	——	——	——

Answer the number of times per year you...

	VSP#	1	2	3	4	5	6
Attend carnivals		___	___	___	___	___	___
Attend high school sporting events		___	___	___	___	___	___
Attend professional sporting events		___	___	___	___	___	___
Change the oil in your car		___	___	___	___	___	___
Fly in a plane		___	___	___	___	___	___
Get your hair cut		___	___	___	___	___	___
Go bowling		___	___	___	___	___	___
Go fishing		___	___	___	___	___	___
Go to the beach		___	___	___	___	___	___
Read a book		___	___	___	___	___	___
Play miniature golf		___	___	___	___	___	___
Play tennis		___	___	___	___	___	___
Go to the movies		___	___	___	___	___	___
Travel over night		___	___	___	___	___	___

FAVORITES

Actors/actresses:

- VSP 1: _____
  _____

- VSP 2: _____
  _____

- VSP 3: _____
  _____

- VSP 4: _____
  _____

- VSP 5: _____
  _____

- VSP 6: _____
  _____

Movies:

- VSP 1: _____
- VSP 2: _____
- VSP 3: _____
- VSP 4: _____
- VSP 5: _____
- VSP 6: _____

Types of movies (horror, comedy, drama, sci-fi, etc.):

- VSP 1: _____
- VSP 2: _____
- VSP 3: _____
- VSP 4: _____
- VSP 5: _____
- VSP 6: _____

TV shows

- VSP 1: _____
- VSP 2: _____
- VSP 3: _____
- VSP 4: _____
- VSP 5: _____
- VSP 6: _____

Singers/bands/musicians:

- VSP 1: _____
- VSP 2: _____
- VSP 3: _____
- VSP 4: _____
- VSP 5: _____
- VSP 6: _____

Painters/photographers/sculptors:

- VSP 1: _____
- VSP 2: _____
- VSP 3: _____
- VSP 4: _____
- VSP 5: _____
- VSP 6: _____

Books and authors:

- VSP 1: _____
- VSP 2: _____
- VSP 3: _____
- VSP 4: _____
- VSP 5: _____
- VSP 6: _____

Magazines/newspapers:

- VSP 1: _____
- VSP 2: _____
- VSP 3: _____
- VSP 4: _____
- VSP 5: _____
- VSP 6: _____

Clothing brands:

- VSP 1: _____
- VSP 2: _____
- VSP 3: _____
- VSP 4: _____
- VSP 5: _____
- VSP 6: _____

Colors to wear:

- VSP 1: _____
- VSP 2: _____
- VSP 3: _____
- VSP 4: _____
- VSP 5: _____
- VSP 6: _____

Colognes/perfumes:

- VSP 1: _____
- VSP 2: _____
- VSP 3: _____
- VSP 4: _____
- VSP 5: _____
- VSP 6: _____

Alcoholic drinks:

- VSP 1: _____
- VSP 2: _____
- VSP 3: _____
- VSP 4: _____
- VSP 5: _____
- VSP 6: _____

Non-alcoholic drinks:

- VSP 1: _____
- VSP 2: _____
- VSP 3: _____
- VSP 4: _____
- VSP 5: _____
- VSP 6: _____

Desserts/sweets:

- VSP 1: _____
- VSP 2: _____
- VSP 3: _____
- VSP 4: _____
- VSP 5: _____
- VSP 6: _____

Main courses:

- VSP 1: _____
- VSP 2: _____
- VSP 3: _____
- VSP 4: _____
- VSP 5: _____
- VSP 6: _____

Fast food restaurants:

- VSP 1: _____
- VSP 2: _____
- VSP 3: _____
- VSP 4: _____
- VSP 5: _____
- VSP 6: _____

Restaurants:

- VSP 1: _____
- VSP 2: _____
- VSP 3: _____
- VSP 4: _____
- VSP 5: _____
- VSP 6: _____

Flowers:

- VSP 1: _____
- VSP 2: _____
- VSP 3: _____
- VSP 4: _____
- VSP 5: _____
- VSP 6: _____

Holidays:

- VSP 1: _____
- VSP 2: _____
- VSP 3: _____
- VSP 4: _____
- VSP 5: _____
- VSP 6: _____

Lucky numbers:

- VSP 1: _____
- VSP 2: _____
- VSP 3: _____
- VSP 4: _____
- VSP 5: _____
- VSP 6: _____

Shopping venues (specific malls, stores, catalogs, websites, etc.)

- VSP 1: _____
- VSP 2: _____
- VSP 3: _____
- VSP 4: _____
- VSP 5: _____
- VSP 6: _____

Sports (participating):

- VSP 1: _____
- VSP 2: _____
- VSP 3: _____
- VSP 4: _____
- VSP 5: _____
- VSP 6: _____

Sports (watching):

- VSP 1: _____
- VSP 2: _____
- VSP 3: _____
- VSP 4: _____
- VSP 5: _____
- VSP 6: _____

Sports teams and athletes:

- VSP 1: _____
- VSP 2: _____
- VSP 3: _____
- VSP 4: _____
- VSP 5: _____
- VSP 6: _____

Tourist attractions and natural wonders:

- VSP 1: _____
- VSP 2: _____
- VSP 3: _____
- VSP 4: _____
- VSP 5: _____
- VSP 6: _____

Vacation spots:

- VSP 1: _____
- VSP 2: _____
- VSP 3: _____
- VSP 4: _____
- VSP 5: _____
- VSP 6: _____

Websites:

- VSP 1: _____
- VSP 2: _____
- VSP 3: _____
- VSP 4: _____
- VSP 5: _____
- VSP 6: _____

PREFERENCES

Select your preference from each line and enter the number below your VSP#.

	VSP#	1	2	3	4	5	6
At a club: 1. Dance 2. Watch		___	___	___	___	___	___
A weekend away: 1. Beach 2. Mountains		___	___	___	___	___	___
The best society: 1. Capitalism 2. Communism 3. Socialism		___	___	___	___	___	___
A restaurant dish: 1. Fish 2. Poultry 3. Red meat 4. Salad		___	___	___	___	___	___
To drink at lunch: 1. Water 2. Soda 3. Tea		___	___	___	___	___	___
Pets: 1. Cats 2. Dogs 3. Fish 4. Birds 5. Rodents 6. Reptiles		___	___	___	___	___	___
Sports: 1. Baseball 2. Basketball 3. Football 4. Hockey 5. Soccer		___	___	___	___	___	___
Flavors: 1. Chocolate 2. Strawberry 3. Vanilla		___	___	___	___	___	___
Jewelry: 1. Gold 2. Platinum 3. Silver 4. White Gold		___	___	___	___	___	___
Where to live: 1. City 2. Country 3. Suburbs		___	___	___	___	___	___
Photos: 1. Black & White 2. Color		___	___	___	___	___	___

	VSP#	1	2	3	4	5	6
In the car: 1. CD/Tape 2. Music radio 3. Talk radio 4. Silence		——	——	——	——	——	——
Bathing: 1. Bath 2. Shower		——	——	——	——	——	——
Sleep: 1.Clothed 2. Unclothed		——	——	——	——	——	——
Sleeping position: 1.Back 2. Side 3. Stomach		——	——	——	——	——	——
Preferred vehicle: 1. Sedan 2.Sports car 3. SUV 4. Truck 5. Van		——	——	——	——	——	——
Seasons: 1. Fall 2. Spring 3. Summer 4. Winter		——	——	——	——	——	——
Beer: 1. Dark 2. Light 3. Medium		——	——	——	——	——	——
Wine: 1. Red 2. White		——	——	——	——	——	——
Pizza: 1. Meat 2. Plain 3. Supreme 4. Veggie 5. White		——	——	——	——	——	——
Plane seating: 1. Aisle 2. Middle 3. Window		——	——	——	——	——	——
Your philosophy: 1. Optimism 2. Pessimism		——	——	——	——	——	——

DREAMS AND DESIRES

Describe your dream house:

- VSP 1: _____

_____

- VSP 2: _____

_____

- VSP 3: _____

_____

- VSP 4: _____

_____

- VSP 5: _____

_____

- VSP 6: _____

_____

List dream jobs you would love to have and why you would love to have them:

- VSP 1: _____

_____

- VSP 2: _____

_____

- VSP 3: _____

_____

- VSP 4: _____

_____

- VSP 5: _____

_____

- VSP 6: _____

_____

List famous people you want to meet and why you would like to meet them:

- VSP 1: _____

_____

- VSP 2: _____

_____

- VSP 3: _____

_____

- VSP 4: _____

_____

- VSP 5: _____

_____

- VSP 6: _____

_____

If a genie appeared to you and gave you three wishes, for what would you ask?

- VSP 1: _____

_____

- VSP 2: _____

_____

- VSP 3: _____

_____

- VSP 4: _____

_____

- VSP 5: _____

_____

- VSP 6: _____

_____

If you could change one thing about your life so far, what would it be?

- VSP 1: _____

_____

- VSP 2: _____

_____

- VSP 3: _____

_____

- VSP 4: _____

_____

- VSP 5: _____

_____

- VSP 6: _____

_____

If you could have the answer to one question, what would that question be?

- VSP 1: _____

_____

- VSP 2: _____

_____

- VSP 3: _____

_____

- VSP 4: _____

_____

- VSP 5: _____

_____

- VSP 6: _____

_____

If you were very wealthy, what charities would you support/found?

- VSP 1: _____
- VSP 2: _____
- VSP 3: _____
- VSP 4: _____
- VSP 5: _____
- VSP 6: _____

If you won the lottery, you would:

- VSP 1: _____
- VSP 2: _____
- VSP 3: _____
- VSP 4: _____
- VSP 5: _____
- VSP 6: _____

List the places to which you would travel if money were no object:

- VSP 1: _____

_____

- VSP 2: _____

_____

- VSP 3: _____

_____

- VSP 4: _____

_____

- VSP 5: _____

_____

- VSP 6: _____

_____

List five things you want to do before you die:

- VSP 1: _____

  _____

- VSP 2: _____

  _____

- VSP 3: _____

  _____

- VSP 4: _____

  _____

- VSP 5: _____

  _____

- VSP 6: _____

  _____

What is your idea of happiness?

- VSP 1: _____

_____

- VSP 2: _____

_____

- VSP 3: _____

_____

- VSP 4: _____

_____

- VSP 5: _____

_____

- VSP 6: _____

_____

DO YOU...

Enter "Y" for Yes and "N" for No below your VSP#.

	VSP#	1	2	3	4	5	6
Arrive late to work often		____	____	____	____	____	____
Bite your nails often		____	____	____	____	____	____
Blow dry your hair regularly		____	____	____	____	____	____
Drive stick shift		____	____	____	____	____	____
Exceed the speed limit regularly		____	____	____	____	____	____
Fall asleep in the car		____	____	____	____	____	____
Garden often		____	____	____	____	____	____
Give blood annually		____	____	____	____	____	____
Hit the snooze button regularly		____	____	____	____	____	____
Keep a daily journal		____	____	____	____	____	____
Own house plants		____	____	____	____	____	____

	VSP#	1	2	3	4	5	6
Read in the bathroom		——	——	——	——	——	——
Read the newspaper daily		——	——	——	——	——	——
Recycle regularly		——	——	——	——	——	——
Send birthday/holiday cards to friends		——	——	——	——	——	——
Set your clock/watch ahead		——	——	——	——	——	——
Sleep walk		——	——	——	——	——	——
Snore regularly		——	——	——	——	——	——
Talk in your sleep		——	——	——	——	——	——
Write letters often		——	——	——	——	——	——

HAVE YOU EVER...

Enter "Y" for Yes and "N" for No below your VSP#.

	VSP#	1	2	3	4	5	6
Asked a "stranger" to dance		——	——	——	——	——	——
Attended a circus		——	——	——	——	——	——
Attended a high school reunion		——	——	——	——	——	——
Been bitten by a strange dog		——	——	——	——	——	——
Been hypnotized		——	——	——	——	——	——
Been stung by a bee		——	——	——	——	——	——
Been to the top of a volcano		——	——	——	——	——	——
Belly danced		——	——	——	——	——	——
Body surfed in the ocean		——	——	——	——	——	——
Boxed		——	——	——	——	——	——

	VSP#	1	2	3	4	5	6
Bungee jumped		——	——	——	——	——	——
Camped in a tent		——	——	——	——	——	——
Canoed/kayaked		——	——	——	——	——	——
Changed an automobile tire		——	——	——	——	——	——
Cheated on a test		——	——	——	——	——	——
Christmas caroled		——	——	——	——	——	——
Created your own web site		——	——	——	——	——	——
Dunked a basketball		——	— —	——	——	——	——
Dyed your hair		——	——	——	——	——	——
Fallen asleep in a class or seminar		——	——	——	——	——	——
Fired a gun		——	——	——	——	——	——
Fished a lake, stream, or river		——	——	——	——	——	——
Fished in the ocean		——	——	——	——	——	——
Flown an airplane		——	——	——	——	——	——
Flown in a helicopter		——	——	——	——	——	——

	VSP#	1	2	3	4	5	6
Flown in a hot air balloon		——	——	——	——	——	——
Flown in an airplane		——	——	——	——	——	——
Flown in First Class on an airplane		——	——	——	——	——	——
Golfed an 18-hole golf course		——	——	——	——	——	——
Gone hang gliding		——	——	——	——	——	——
Gone on a Safari		——	——	——	——	——	——
Gone rock climbing		——	——	——	——	——	——
Gone sky diving		——	——	——	——	——	——
Had your heart broken		——	——	——	——	——	——
Had your palm read		——	——	——	——	——	——
Held a snake		——	——	——	——	——	——
Hiked on the Appalachian Trail		——	——	——	——	——	——
Hit an animal in the road with your car		——	——	——	——	——	——
Hit someone with your fist forcefully		——	——	——	——	——	——
Hitchhiked		——	——	——	——	——	——

	VSP#	1	2	3	4	5	6
Hunted							
Jet skied							
Jumped on a trampoline							
Knitted							
Laughed so hard you cried							
Laughed so hard your drink came out your nose							
Learned a martial art							
Learned sign language							
Learned yoga							
Marched in a parade							
Modeled							
Painted a painting							
Parasailed							
Participated in a séance							
Passed out from drinking							

	VSP#	1	2	3	4	5	6
Played poker		——	——	——	——	——	——
Received a massage at a spa		——	——	——	——	——	——
Ridden a horse		——	——	——	——	——	——
Ridden a motorcycle		——	——	——	——	——	——
Ridden a snowmobile		——	——	——	——	——	——
Ridden in a big city taxi		——	——	——	——	——	——
Ridden the subway/train		——	——	——	——	——	——
Rollerbladed		——	——	——	——	——	——
Run in a marathon		——	——	——	——	——	——
Sailed on a sail boat		——	——	——	——	——	——
Sat in on a session of the Senate or the House		——	——	——	——	——	——
Sat on a jury		——	——	——	——	——	——
Saved someone's life		——	——	——	——	——	——
SCUBA dived		——	——	——	——	——	——
Sculpted a sculpture		——	——	——	——	——	——

	VSP#	1	2	3	4	5	6
Seen a shark in the wild		—	—	—	—	—	—
Seen a whale in the wild		—	—	—	—	—	—
Sighted a UFO		—	—	—	—	—	—
Skied		—	—	—	—	—	—
Skinny dipped		—	—	—	—	—	—
Skipped school		—	—	—	—	—	—
Slept on the beach all night		—	—	—	—	—	—
Smoked cigarettes regularly		—	—	—	—	—	—
Snorkeled a reef		—	—	—	—	—	—
Snowboarded		—	—	—	—	—	—
Soiled your pants		—	—	—	—	—	—
Spent a summer at the ocean		—	—	—	—	—	—
Spent the night in jail		—	—	—	—	—	—
Stayed up all night		—	—	—	—	—	—
Surfed on a real surf board		—	—	—	—	—	—

	VSP#	1	2	3	4	5	6
Sung in front of a mirror		——	——	——	——	——	——
Sung/Karaoke in public		——	——	——	——	——	——
Taken a cruise		——	——	——	——	——	——
Taught a class/seminar		——	——	——	——	——	——
Taught your dog tricks		——	——	——	——	——	——
Visited a nude beach		——	——	——	——	——	——
Water skied		——	——	——	——	——	——
Whitewater rafted		——	——	——	——	——	——

HAVE YOU BEEN...

Enter "Y" for Yes and "N" for No below your VSP#.

	VSP#	1	2	3	4	5	6
Acadia National Park in Maine		___	___	___	___	___	___
Arches - Canyonlands National Parks in Utah		___	___	___	___	___	___
Carlsbad Caverns National Park in New Mexico		___	___	___	___	___	___
Colonial Williamsburg in Williamsburg, VA		___	___	___	___	___	___
Daytona International Speedway in Daytona, FL		___	___	___	___	___	___
Denali National Park in Alaska		___	___	___	___	___	___
Everglades National Park in Florida		___	___	___	___	___	___
Glacier National Park in Montana		___	___	___	___	___	___
Graceland in Memphis, TN		___	___	___	___	___	___
Haleakala volcanic crater in Haleakala, HI		___	___	___	___	___	___
Independence National Historical Park in Philadelphia, PA		___	___	___	___	___	___

	VSP#	1	2	3	4	5	6
Mount Rushmore in Keystone, SD		——	——	——	——	——	——
Niagara Falls in Niagara Falls, NY		——	——	——	——	——	——
Pearl Harbor in Honolulu, HI		——	——	——	——	——	——
Rocky Mountain National Park in Colorado		——	——	——	——	——	——
South Beach in Miami, FL		——	——	——	——	——	——
Stone Mountain State Park in Stone Mountain, GA		——	——	——	——	——	——
The "Grassy Knoll" in Dallas, TX		——	——	——	——	——	——
The beaches of the US Virgin Islands		——	——	——	——	——	——
The Big Sur Coast in California		——	——	——	——	——	——
The Freedom Trail in Boston, MA		——	——	——	——	——	——
The French Quarter in New Orleans, LA		——	——	——	——	——	——
The Gateway Arch in St. Louis, MO		——	——	——	——	——	——
The Golden Gate Bridge in San Francisco, CA		——	——	——	——	——	——
The Grand Canyon in Arizona		——	——	——	——	——	——
The Grand Ole Opry in Nashville, TN		——	——	——	——	——	——

	VSP#	1	2	3	4	5	6
The Hollywood studios in Hollywood, CA		——	——	——	——	——	——
The Mall of America in Bloomington, MN		——	——	——	——	——	——
The National Mall and monuments in Washington, DC		——	——	——	——	——	——
The Outer Banks in North Carolina		——	——	——	——	——	——
The Pro Baseball Hall of Fame in Cooperstown, NY		——	——	——	——	——	——
The Pro Football Hall of Fame in Akron, OH		——	——	——	——	——	——
The River Walk in San Antonio, TX		——	——	——	——	——	——
The San Diego Zoo in San Diego, CA		——	——	——	——	——	——
The Sears Tower Skydeck in Chicago, IL		——	——	——	——	——	——
The Space Needle in Seattle, WA		——	——	——	——	——	——
The Statue of Liberty in New York, NY		——	——	——	——	——	——
The Strip in Las Vegas, NV		——	——	——	——	——	——
Walt Disney World in Orlando, FL		——	——	——	——	——	——
Yellowstone-Grant Teton National Parks in Wyoming		——	——	——	——	——	——
Yosemite National Park in California		——	——	——	——	——	——

BELIEFS

What religion were you raised and/or do you practice?

- VSP 1: _____

_____

- VSP 2: _____

_____

- VSP 3: _____

_____

- VSP 4: _____

_____

- VSP 5: _____

_____

- VSP 6: _____

_____

Do you believe in God? Explain your answer:

- VSP 1: _____

  _____

- VSP 2: _____

  _____

- VSP 3: _____

  _____

- VSP 4: _____

  _____

- VSP 5: _____

  _____

- VSP 6: _____

  _____

Describe what the Bible is to you:

- VSP 1: _____

_____

- VSP 2: _____

_____

- VSP 3: _____

_____

- VSP 4: _____

_____

- VSP 5: _____

_____

- VSP 6: _____

_____

Do you believe in an afterlife? If so, describe it:

- VSP 1: _____

_____

- VSP 2: _____

_____

- VSP 3: _____

_____

- VSP 4: _____

_____

- VSP 5: _____

_____

- VSP 6: _____

_____

Do only Christians go to heaven? Explain your answer:

- VSP 1: _____

_____

- VSP 2: _____

_____

- VSP 3: _____

_____

- VSP 4: _____

_____

- VSP 5: _____

_____

- VSP 6: _____

_____

Do you believe in UFO's and/or life on other planets? Explain your answer:

- VSP 1: _____

_____

- VSP 2: _____

_____

- VSP 3: _____

_____

- VSP 4: _____

_____

- VSP 5: _____

_____

- VSP 6: _____

_____

Do you believe in ghosts? Explain your answer:

- VSP 1: _____

_____

- VSP 2: _____

_____

- VSP 3: _____

_____

- VSP 4: _____

_____

- VSP 5: _____

_____

- VSP 6: _____

_____

What are your thoughts on premarital sex?

- VSP 1: _____

_____

- VSP 2: _____

_____

- VSP 3: _____

_____

- VSP 4: _____

_____

- VSP 5: _____

_____

- VSP 6: _____

_____

POLITICAL VIEWS

What is your political party affiliation and why are you affiliated in this manner?

- VSP 1: _____

_____

- VSP 2: _____

_____

- VSP 3: _____

_____

- VSP 4: _____

_____

- VSP 5: _____

_____

- VSP 6: _____

_____

If you became President tomorrow, what are the 3 things about the US Government you would change?

- VSP 1: _____

_____

- VSP 2: _____

_____

- VSP 3: _____

_____

- VSP 4: _____

_____

- VSP 5: _____

_____

- VSP 6: _____

_____

POLITICAL YES NO

Enter "Y" for Yes and "N" for No beside your VSP#.

Should smoking be banned in all indoor public places?

     VSP 1_____ VSP 2_____ VSP 3_____ VSP 4_____ VSP 5_____ VSP 6_____

Do you support the NASA space flight program?

     VSP 1_____ VSP 2_____ VSP 3_____ VSP 4_____ VSP 5_____ VSP 6_____

Should pornography be censored on the internet?

     VSP 1_____ VSP 2_____ VSP 3_____ VSP 4_____ VSP 5_____ VSP 6_____

Should the private sale of guns be subject to background checks like all other legal gun sales?

     VSP 1_____ VSP 2_____ VSP 3_____ VSP 4_____ VSP 5_____ VSP 6_____

Do you support waiting periods for gun purchases?

     VSP 1_____ VSP 2_____ VSP 3_____ VSP 4_____ VSP 5_____ VSP 6_____

Do you support the "3 strikes" rule (3 felony convictions results in a mandatory life sentence)?

VSP 1_____ VSP 2_____ VSP 3_____ VSP 4_____ VSP 5_____ VSP 6_____

Are you in favor of a two party system or would you like to see a third or fourth major political party?

VSP 1_____ VSP 2_____ VSP 3_____ VSP 4_____ VSP 5_____ VSP 6_____

Do you usually vote a straight ticket (pull the lever for one party)?

VSP 1_____ VSP 2_____ VSP 3_____ VSP 4_____ VSP 5_____ VSP 6_____

Should people near death that are in unbearable pain be allowed to die through medically assisted life termination?

VSP 1_____ VSP 2_____ VSP 3_____ VSP 4_____ VSP 5_____ VSP 6_____

Should the government ensure that all qualifying students can attend college by providing student aid such as loans and grants?

VSP 1_____ VSP 2_____ VSP 3_____ VSP 4_____ VSP 5_____ VSP 6_____

Should the government promote a low-cost online university that allows students to study at home and take tests locally?

VSP 1_____ VSP 2_____ VSP 3_____ VSP 4_____ VSP 5_____ VSP 6_____

Should "white collar" criminals receive harsh sentences (20yrs-life), especially in the case of "crimes against society" that affect hundreds or thousands of people?

VSP 1_____ VSP 2_____ VSP 3_____ VSP 4_____ VSP 5_____ VSP 6_____

Should school (K-9) students be required to pass a standardized test to "graduate" to the next grade level?

VSP 1_____ VSP 2_____ VSP 3_____ VSP 4_____ VSP 5_____ VSP 6_____

Do you believe that citizens that make more money should pay a higher percent of taxes on income?

VSP 1_____ VSP 2_____ VSP 3_____ VSP 4_____ VSP 5_____ VSP 6_____

Federal Estate Tax is a "redistribution of wealth" via taxing "large" estates (currently estates over $1.5 million). Do you agree with the Estate Tax?

VSP 1_____ VSP 2_____ VSP 3_____ VSP 4_____ VSP 5_____ VSP 6_____

Do you support the death penalty?

VSP 1_____ VSP 2_____ VSP 3_____ VSP 4_____ VSP 5_____ VSP 6_____

Should abortion be allowed under special circumstances such as in the case of rape or incest, if the fetus is deformed, or when the mother's life is in question?

VSP 1_____ VSP 2_____ VSP 3_____ VSP 4_____ VSP 5_____ VSP 6_____

Should abortion be legal in the first trimester (the fetus grows to approximately 2.5 inches long and 1 ounce in weight)?

VSP 1_____ VSP 2_____ VSP 3_____ VSP 4_____ VSP 5_____ VSP 6_____

Should abortion be legal in the 2nd trimester (the fetus grows to approximately 1 foot long and 1 pound in weight)?

VSP 1_____ VSP 2_____ VSP 3_____ VSP 4_____ VSP 5_____ VSP 6_____

Should eligible candidates' campaigns be publicly funded rather than allowing contributions from special interest groups?

VSP 1_____ VSP 2_____ VSP 3_____ VSP 4_____ VSP 5_____ VSP 6_____

Are you in favor of the use of referendum voting (direct popular vote on issues)?

VSP 1_____ VSP 2_____ VSP 3_____ VSP 4_____ VSP 5_____ VSP 6_____

Should the government ensure equal results for minorities through quotas (the alternative is to ensure equal opportunity)?

VSP 1_____ VSP 2_____ VSP 3_____ VSP 4_____ VSP 5_____ VSP 6_____

Should our government balance the budget?

VSP 1_____ VSP 2_____ VSP 3_____ VSP 4_____ VSP 5_____ VSP 6_____

Should homosexuals be allowed to adopt children?

VSP 1_____ VSP 2_____ VSP 3_____ VSP 4_____ VSP 5_____ VSP 6_____

Should homosexual couples be allowed to apply for "civil union" so that they receive similar benefits as married heterosexuals?

VSP 1_____ VSP 2_____ VSP 3_____ VSP 4_____ VSP 5_____ VSP 6_____

Would legalizing some drugs such as marijuana destroy the black market and reduce crime?

VSP 1_____ VSP 2_____ VSP 3_____ VSP 4_____ VSP 5_____ VSP 6_____

Should the government focus on promoting English as the official language of our country?

VSP 1_____ VSP 2_____ VSP 3_____ VSP 4_____ VSP 5_____ VSP 6_____

Should all citizens have equal access to health care?

VSP 1_____ VSP 2_____ VSP 3_____ VSP 4_____ VSP 5_____ VSP 6_____

Should doctors be allowed to charge citizens with no health insurance higher fees than they charge the insurance companies/insured customers?

VSP 1_____ VSP 2_____ VSP 3_____ VSP 4_____ VSP 5_____ VSP 6_____

Should the government support stem cell research?

VSP 1_____ VSP 2_____ VSP 3_____ VSP 4_____ VSP 5_____ VSP 6_____

Should cloning of human organs be banned?

VSP 1_____ VSP 2_____ VSP 3_____ VSP 4_____ VSP 5_____ VSP 6_____

Should the current Social Security system be replaced with mandatory individual retirement accounts similar to IRA's?

VSP 1_____ VSP 2_____ VSP 3_____ VSP 4_____ VSP 5_____ VSP 6_____

ORDER ADDITIONAL COPIES OF THE BOOK...

Save 20%-50% on bulk orders...
Visit our website at www.CSManifold.com

- o   If you have more VSP's you would like to learn about.
- o   To be given as token gifts for business associates and customers.
- o   As a gift for friends and family, any time of the year including Christmas, Hanukah, Mother's Day, Father's Day, Valentine's Day, weddings, birthdays, graduations, etc.
- o   To be used to raise funds for charity, non-profit organizations, schools, etc.
- o   As a means to earn extra money as an independent sales representative.

	# of copies		Price	Total
Knowing Me, Knowing You (paperback version)	_____	X	$11.99	$_____
Shipping Charge				$ 1.99
Net Total..				$_____
Virginia residents please add 5% sales tax....................				$_____
Total...				$_____

Make your check or money
order payable and return to:

To the Point Publishing
P.O. Box 10799
Burke, Va 22009-0799

For credit card orders visit us
on the web at
www.CSManifold.com

Name _____

Address/City/State/Zip_____

Phone # _____   E-mail _____

Knowing Me, Knowing You   "A Biography of You and Your Loved Ones"